stardoll™

Fame, fashion and friends

OFFICIAL
HANDBOOK
Every girl's must-have guide!

BANTAM BOOKS

Fame, fashion and friends

**We hope you have lots of fun joining in the Stardoll world.
Remember to be safe online and never give out your Stardoll password,
email addresses, or any other personal information, including photos.**

STARDOLL: OFFICIAL HANDBOOK
A BANTAM BOOK 978 0 857 51079 2

First published in Great Britain by Bantam,
an imprint of Random House Children's Books
A Random House Group Company.

This edition published 2011

1 3 5 7 9 10 8 6 4 2

STARDOLL © 2011 Stardoll AB. All Rights Reserved. www.stardoll.com

Stardoll.com is an ever-evolving website. This book was released in September 2011;
however, please be aware that updates and changes may have happened on
Stardoll.com since then.

Exclusive Stardoll virtual gift can be found by locating the code and
instructions within the pages of this book. Gift codes can be redeemed
until the expiry date, 31/12/2012

Produced by Shubrook Bros. Creative
www.shubrookbros.com
With special thanks to Paul Terry, Julia Hardy and Caroline Askew

P13 © Rex Features, © Richard Young / Rex Features, © Richard Young / Rex Features, ©
Agencia EFE / Rex Features, © Startraks Photo / Rex Features

Bantam Books are published by Random House Children's Books,
61–63 Uxbridge Road, London W5 5SA

www.**kids**a**t**r**andomhouse**.co.uk
www.**totally**r**andombooks**.co.uk
www.**randomhouse**.co.uk

Addresses for companies within The Random House Group Limited can be found at:
www.randomhouse.co.uk/offices.htm

THE RANDOM HOUSE GROUP Limited Reg. No. 954009

A CIP catalogue record for this book is available from the British Library.

Printed in Italy

BANTAM
BOOKS

CONTENTS

Let's get Creative!

Hi Stardolls — Callie here! I'm so thrilled you've picked up this complete guide to the stylish world of Stardoll.

We love making friends, sharing ideas and celebrating being an individual. The way you express yourself is what we love the most at Stardoll!

In this Handbook I'll talk you through everything you can do on Stardoll, from making your all-important MeDoll and designing contest-winning styles, to making fab fashion friends from around the globe.

On the website I'm at Callie.Stardoll, so come and say hi! My 'Quick Facts' are on the right — and I'll be asking you to complete a 'Quick Facts' box in a sec too.

But that's enough about me — now it's over to you. Let's get creative!

Twinkle, twinkle,

Callie x

TOP tips

Before you get started on Stardoll, remember to check out the Stardoll Code Of Conduct. You can find this important 'Etiquette' guide under the 'Help' bar.

CALLIE'S QUICKFACTS

Celebrity look-a-like: Zoe Saldana

Favourite celebrity: Madonna

Favourite music: All kinds

Favourite movie: Comedy

Favourite food: Ice cream

Favourite colour: Black

Future dream job: Designing clothes

Favourite TV show: Project Runway

Eye colour: Brown

Hair colour: Brunette

Spending my time with: Real life friends

MAKING YOUR MEDOLL!

This is where the fashion fun really begins! But before we talk you through how to create your MeDoll (or AvaStar as we also like to call them), let's find out more about you. Your favourite things will really help you come up with some amazing ideas for your MeDoll's style!

(Activity) ## It Starts With You

Print out a photo that you really love, cut it out and glue it in the box on the right. It could be you out with your friends, or just you in your favourite outfit, whatever you like!

STICK YOUR PHOTO HERE!

Your QuickFacts

Just like on Callie's welcome page, fill in the blanks to create a fun summary of things about you. Try chatting with your friends if you're having trouble deciding on which answers best reflect you.

STICK YOUR CELEBRITY PICTURE HERE!

Celebrity look-a-like:
cherl cole

Favourite celebrity:
pixie lot

Favourite music:
All kinds

Favourite movie:
Horror

Favourite food:
pizza

Favourite colour:
Black

Future dream job:
singer

Favourite TV-show:
project runaway

Eye colour:
BrowN

Hair colour:
Brundie

Spending my time with:
friends

Activity

My Fashion Idol

Love Cheryl Cole's style? Obsessed with Katy Perry's outrageous outfits? Pick a fave celeb, cut out a picture you love of them and stick it on the right.

Now let's find out what you love about this star's style:

What is your favourite outfit or accessory of theirs?

..... Hair , cloths .....

What colour do you think looks the best on them?

..... purple .....

What do you love about the way they wear their hair?

..... It is so pritty .....

If you could create any outfit or accessory for your idol, what would it be and why?

..... dont n .....

..... dont no .....

STICK YOUR CELEBRITY PICTURE HERE!

THE AMAZING MEDOLL

Your MeDoll is as unique as you are! There are over 60 billion variations with an almost endless range of hairstyles, clothes and accessories! Plus, more can be tried on and bought from the Starplaza! But it doesn't end there. You can create suites, photo albums, pet pals, parties . . . your MeDoll is your passport to friends, fashion and getting creative!

BODY, FACE, NOSE & LIPS!

Activity

If you love a trend of your own, your friends' or from the celeb world, the MeDoll is your chance to take that inspiration and start experimenting!

BODY SHAPE

1

Here are some of the BODY types available to choose from on Stardoll. Try sketching some outfits for each of them.

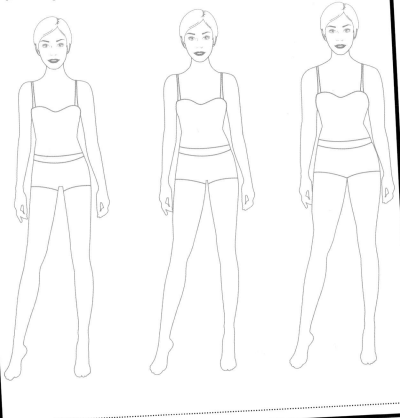

FACE SHAPE

2

Do you like strong features or a delicate FACE? Use a pencil to try out some shapes you'd like your MeDoll to have.

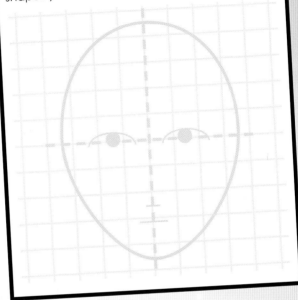

NOSE & LIPS

3

Your NOSE and LIPS options include the below. Circle which one you'd like for your MeDoll.

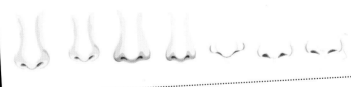

What are your favourite lipstick shades? Colour these lips in to get some ideas for your MeDoll.

HAIRSTYLES

Activity

Your MeDoll is really starting to take shape.
Now it's time to have your hairdryers,
brushes and products at the ready!

Fancy yourself as a bit of a hairstylist? First of all, check out these
MeDoll hair types below and give them some Starpoints – the
more the points, the more you love the 'do! Then make some
notes below about why they rock your style world.

1

2

3

2

1

2

My favourite styles are... number 1 and number 3 on top row

Because...

Here you can experiment with the colour choices for your MeDoll hair too. Grab some colouring pens or pencils and get styling:

Activity

Your Styles So Far

So those are your fave hairdos for your MeDoll, but what about you?

What hairstyles have you had so far and why?

....

What's been your favourite look on you so far and why?

....

Which of your fashion idols have inspired your hairstyles?

....

EYES & EYEBROWS

Getting some great ideas of how you'd like your MeDoll to look?
You've just got the expressive eyes and eyebrows to decide
upon! There are dozens of options to choose from on Stardoll.
Circle your faves below!

Activity

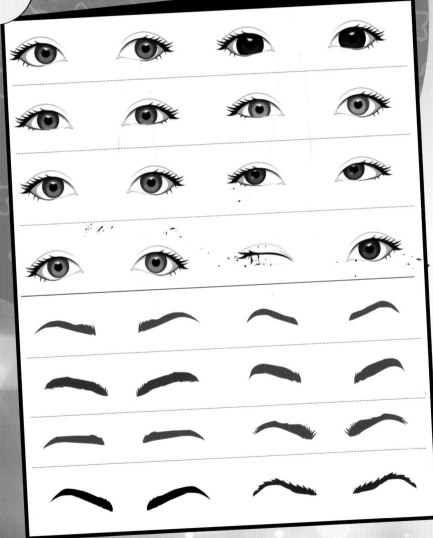

Whose Peepers?

Can you identify the famous eyes? Write down your answers and complete the box below too:

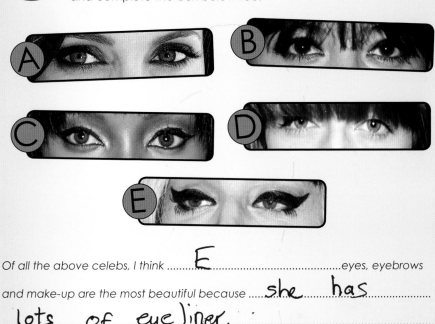

Of all the above celebs, I think ....E................................eyes, eyebrows

and make-up are the most beautiful because .....she has..............

...lots of eye liner...

....

Friends' Awesome Eyes

Who do you know who has an incredible eye for making their lashes luscious? Make a note to help inspire your MeDoll design.

I think ....eyes, eyebrows and make-up are the most

beautiful because...

....

....

GO MAKE YOUR MEDOLL

Now go for it – jump onto Stardoll.com and make your MeDoll! Then, print a copy of it out and stick it below.

STICK YOUR MEDOLL
PICTURE HERE!

TOP tips

Remember, if you want to change your style or look any time, you can in the Beauty Parlour. More on that a bit later (on page 24).

You & Your MeDoll

How similar is your MeDoll to your own style? Has it ended up more like your style idol? Complete the quiz to find out!

	MY STYLE	MY STYLE IDOL	MY MEDOLL
Eye Colour	Brown	Blue	blue
Hair Colour	Brown	black	blond
Hair Style	long	wavy	side
Lipstick Shade	light	red	red

Your MeDoll has got a great look so far! From this point on the fun really begins, as your MeDoll is your passport to a whole world of fashion and creativity! Turn the page — let's get started!

Fame, Fashion & Friends *await you!*

Stardoll is bursting with amazing experiences. We love celeb styles, making great friends, living and breathing everything about the fashion world – and ultimately, getting super-creative with it. Sound like your thing too? Below is what we're about to take you on a tour of: the Starplaza and beyond!

COVERGIRL

Covergirl

Primp my Pet

Games

Starplaza

starplaza

Parties

Suites

YOU LOOK GREAT

starplaza

Starcoins

Pets

Seasonal Sensations

Before we go through the doors of the Starplaza, let's get your mind fizzing with fashion possibilities. Grab your favourite magazines and cut out some examples of looks and trends that you really love right now. Accessories you can never live without? New trends you want to try out? Go!

STICK YOUR
PICTURES IN HERE!

Money for your MeDoll

Once you've created your MeDoll, you'll receive Starcoins to spend on clothes, accessories, furnishings, whatever you like! If you feel like diving even deeper into Stardoll, using Stardollars as a Superstar might suit you and your ideas.

Need-to-know

You can earn Starcoins through playing on Stardoll! The more creative you get, the more Stardoll rewards you for it!

Need-to-know

Becoming a Stardoll Superstar means you can design and sell clothes! Check out p30 for more.

Need-to-know

Starcoins is the main currency, but Stardollars can be bought by Superstar members. They can be used for special purchases like make-up!

Your Favourite Spends

What do you like buying on the high street? Take this quiz to help you work out what you'd like to use your Starcoins for. There are no right or wrong answers, it's all about what works for you!

1. *Which items do you most like shopping for?*

A. Shoes
B. Tops/Shirts
C. Skirts
D. Dresses
E. Accessories

2. *In the wonderful world of shoes, which do you love the most?*

A. Flats
B. Wedges
C. High heels
D. Boots
E. Trainers

3. *What do you like to buy to decorate your bedroom?*

A. Posters
B. Photo frames
C. Flowers
D. Soft toys
E. Figurines

Now, why not jot down an idea or design for one of the above, just to keep those creative juices flowing!

My ideas sketchpad:

Let's go Shopping

Chosen a fab hair style and make-up look for your MeDoll? Not sure what to wear? Well, with the purchasing power of Starcoins, your fashion dreams can come true. Just step inside the doors of the Starplaza and beyond!

Try Everything On!

Everyone can try on clothes without spending ANY Starcoins! So make sure you really do have a full-on Starplaza window shopping experience. Superstar members will discover access to extra things like even more collections.

Grab That

A shopping spree couldn't be easier – everything is clearly priced in Starcoins and Stardollars. There are so many bargains, you'll be able to pick up on-trend accessories for your MeDoll with the click of a button!

Dress To Impress

From leggings and lipsticks, to brogues and boyfriend blazers, the Starplaza is bursting with inspiring fashion, gorgeous beauty products and delicious décors!

Activity

Find Your Fashion Passion

Not sure where to begin browsing the Starplaza shelves? Let's find out what your fave items are:

Q: How would your ultimate bedroom look?

....
....
....

Q: Who is your number one style icon?

....
....
....

Q: What is your favourite look this season and why?

....
....
....

Q: What pieces would you need to recreate that look?

....
....
....

Q: With Starcoins as a present, what's the first thing you'd buy?

....
....
....

Now, keep in mind those fashion faves. If you turn the page, we'll explore the dazzling corridors of the Starplaza!

Shops & Brands

There's such a stunning array of shops and ever-changing clothes to choose from that you'll never be short of trends and ideas for fashion!

Antidote

TOP tips

Whatever you buy will appear in a lovely shopping bag in your Suite, ready to unpack and store away in your wardrobe. Look out for special gifts appearing from Stardoll from time to time too!

Basics

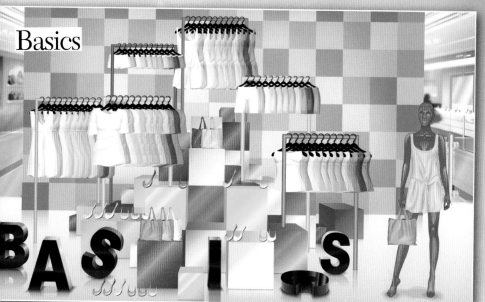

LE – Limited Edition

TOP tips

Stardoll release Limited Edition collections that are HUGELY popular. Check back on the site regularly for them!

Activity Fave So Far?

Which of these collections is most appealing to you? Why not get together with your friends and discuss what you like the most about them, then swap ideas about how to dress your MeDoll. When you've shortlisted some styles, hit the Starplaza and start trying them on!

Beauty Parlour: Make-up

You can have loads of fun trying out make-up styles in the Beauty shops at Starplaza!

Once you've bought your make-up, you can access the Beauty Parlour via your Suite. Give your MeDoll a glamorous makeover as many times as you like!

TOP tips

Want to pick your favourite tried-out looks, take them to the Beauty Parlour, create new ones and save them? Check out being a Superstar on p30.

Eyeliners & Eye Shadows

Blushes

Lipsticks

TOP tips

Love the idea of playing around with different hair accessories? Pop to the Starplaza and get shopping!

Activity Grab some colouring pens or pencils and try out some make-up styles. Be bold and try any colours you like!

Beauty Parlour:
Hands & Nails

Stardoll's nail bar gives you the chance to make your MeDoll's hands as individual as you are. Long, decorated nails, short and simple, it's up to you! Have a practise here on how you'd like your MeDoll's nail art to look. Then, take a trip to Starplaza and have a go at trying out the looks you come up with. Get painting!

Activity

Amazing Nail Art
Multi-coloured? Dark and Gothic? Bright and sunny? You decide!

Activity: Nail Jewellery

It doesn't stop with just using nail varnish – check out the extra art you can add. Circle your faves here!

Unpack *that* Shopping

Not only do you get a unique AvaStar to style, but you also get an incredible Suite to make your own!

Think of your absolute dream hang-out zone: you can completely customize **WALL COLOURS**, **STORAGE** and **WARDROBES**. Plus, there's a huge amount of **DECORATIONS**, **POSTERS** and **FURNITURE** you can get from the **SUITE STORE** – easy to access from inside your Suite. Check out these beautiful items . . .

Cushions

Furniture

Posters

Your Bedroom's Style

Activity

Would you like your Suite to be just like your bedroom?
Or maybe the dream room you've always wanted?
Complete the following to get some more ideas.

My bedroom has ....coloured walls.

On them I've got .... and ....

My favourite piece of furniture is ....

.... Of everything that's in my room, my .... is most

precious to me because ....

My best friends' rooms are different because ....

.... but they have similar things to mine like ....

....

If I could change three things about my bedroom I would:

1)...

2)...

3)...

SUPERSTAR STYLING!

Are you the kind of fashionista who would like to do even more on Stardoll? Things like design and sell clothes for Stardollars? Well, if that's how you'd like to express your creativity, becoming a Superstar could be for you.

Superstar-shaped Things:

- Full access to the Styling Studio
- Play dress-up games and activities
- StarDesign your own line of clothes
- Sell your creations in StarBazaar
- Live like a Superstar in your superior Suite
- Adopt lovable pets: puppies, kittens & more
- Transform your doll with fabulous make-up
- Give your friends luxury gifts
- Host your own fabulous parties

Luxury gifts

GIFT SHOP

MY SUITE

More rooms

Live like a Superstar

Host parties

CREATE A PARTY

Cool make-up

Styling studio

As a Superstar, you can take your MeDoll and make it into a dress-up doll in the Styling Studio. You can control all of the elements, from outfits to locations. What's more, you can then show the rest of the Stardoll world what you've created!

Dress-ups

Locations

TOP tips

Choose which background and which clothes in your closet you want to include and then others can style your MeDoll too!

Enter the studio

Superstars can enter the Styling Studio via the 'Dress-ups & Games' area. There you can restyle your MeDoll, plus do all of this . . .

1 Take clothes onto the rail

2 Pick a room

3 Dress-up, then add to your album

TOP tips

Don't forget, you can also decorate your Album full of your fave stylings!

HAVE A GET-TOGETHER
WITH YOUR FRIENDS
AND MAKE IT A
'STYLING STUDIO' DAY
IN YOUR ROOM . . .

. . . AND USE THESE
SPACES TO STICK IN
YOUR FAVOURITE
PHOTOS FROM THE
'FASHION SHOW'
THAT YOU PUT ON!

Activity
Your Dress-Up Idols
Jot down the top 3 celeb looks you'd love to mimic with your MeDoll!

Celeb 1) ....

Celeb 2) ....

Celeb 3) ....

Dress-up heroes!

With 'fancy dress' being the most fun kind of dressing up, you didn't think Stardoll would forget about it did you? There are hundreds of fancy dress outfits to try out, from your fave actors, to fashion icons throughout history, like the stunning Egyptian princess Cleopatra!

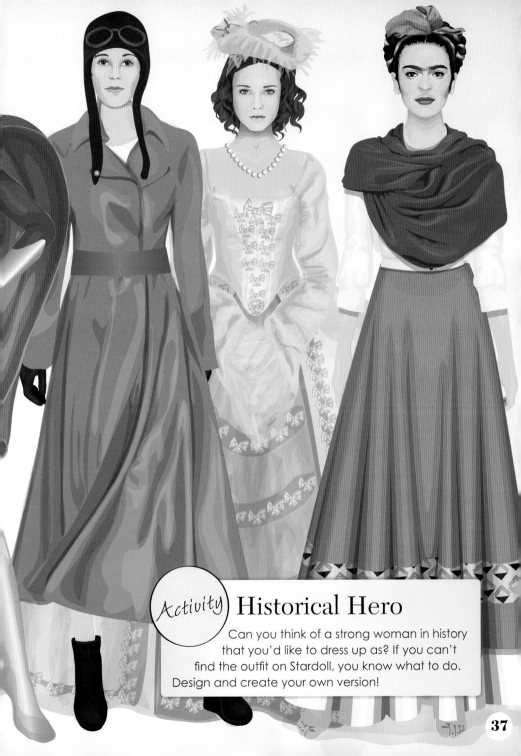

$\overline{Activity}$ Historical Hero

Can you think of a strong woman in history
that you'd like to dress up as? If you can't
find the outfit on Stardoll, you know what to do.
Design and create your own version!

TAKE PART
& EARN STARCOINS!

Now you've seen some of the amazing things you can spend your Starcoins on, wouldn't it be great if your activity on Stardoll actually earned you more coins? It does!

The more interactive your Stardoll experience becomes, the more Starcoins you earn! It's our way of thanking you for being such an important part of Stardoll! Giving you Starcoins in return means you can get even more out of your friendships and fashion experience!

Voting for favourite designs, MeDolls and Albums all earns you Starcoins and Starpoints. You can see just how much you're earning on your special profile page.

COVERGIRL

Vote for Covergirl

TOP tips

Hop on Stardoll and take part in everything on this page, and tick the box when you've done it. Great job!

Rate scenery

Rate an album

Vote best design

Vote best outfit

DESIGN & SELL

Making and dressing your MeDoll is just the beginning of your fashion life on Stardoll. If you do decide to try out being a Superstar, you can also make your own clothing lines in StarDesign and then sell them for Stardollars in StarBazaar!

TOP tips

Like the idea of selling your own designs in StarBazaar? Pop to p44 to find out more about Superstar stylin'.

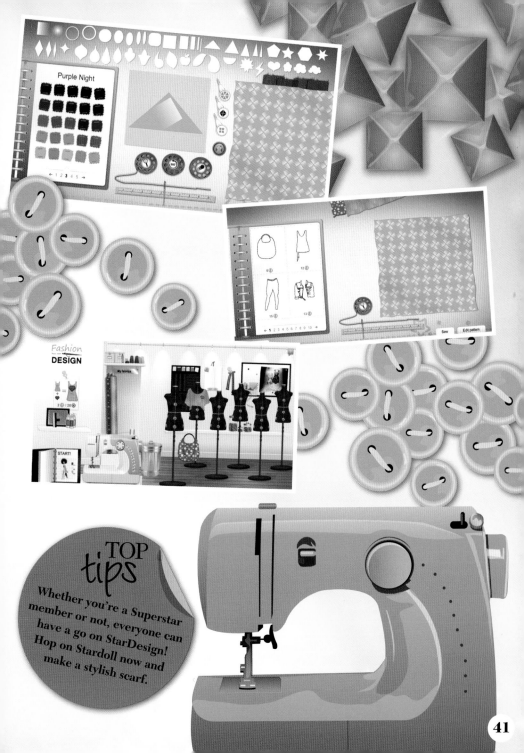

Purple Night

Fashion
DESIGN

TOP tips

Whether you're a Superstar member or not, everyone can have a go on StarDesign! Hop on Stardoll now and make a stylish scarf.

41

Design Your Own Fabric Pattern!

Activity

Here's an example of what your StarDesign studio looks like on Stardoll. First of all, draw your own special shapes in the empty boxes below the colour swatches. Then, use the sketchpad to come up with your own fabric pattern. Once you're done, see what your friends came up with in their Handbooks too!

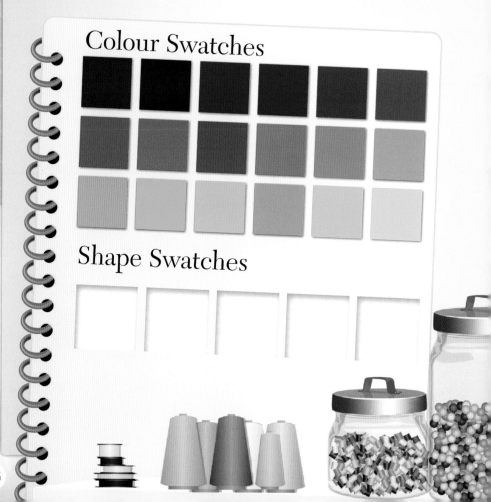

Colour Swatches

Shape Swatches

Sketchpad:

TOP
tips

Look around on Stardoll
and see if any other
members' designs give
you inspiration
for yours.

STARBAZAAR:
THE *vintage* SHOP

In the vintage shop StarBazaar, you can buy clothes and furniture that Superstar members have sold! It's a great way of refreshing your Suite's wardrobe of looks that you're no longer into – but they'll probably inspire another member, so recycle and reap the rewards!

Renew your wardrobe

TOP tips

If you want to practise what it would be like to become a fashion seller, Superstar members can buy and sell in the StarBazaar at any time!

Update your furniture

(Activity) Swap parties!

Why not use the StarBazaar approach to fashion in the physical world! You could have regular parties with your friends where you swap old clothes, accessories and belongings that you're not into anymore, and really inspire each other with new looks!

Style your Suite

Your Suite is where you live on Stardoll – and it's completely up to you how you want it to look! All decorating takes is a combination of your brilliant design ideas and a trip to the Suite Shop to gather what you need.

TOP tips

Remember, you can access the Suite Shop (to deck out your room with brand new items) via your Suite.

Activity Dream Room

Remember the quiz activity
about your own bedroom back
on page 29? See anything here
that fits the style of your dream apartment?
Circle them, find them on Stardoll, and add
them to your AvaStar's Suite!

Different designs

Activity

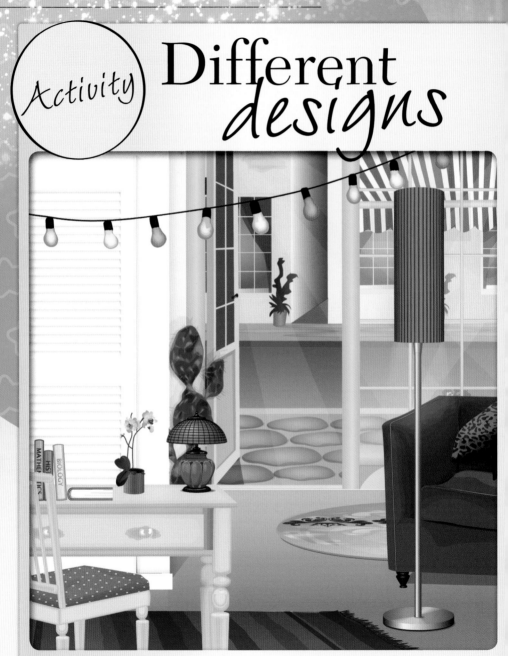

Two identical Stardoll Suites – or are they? Look very closely at them and then list the differences you can spot!

1) ....
2) ....
3) ....
4) ....
5) ....

6) ....
7) ....
8) ....
9) ....
10) ....

Pet Pals

From cats and dogs, to snakes and dolphins, there is a huge range of fun-loving furry pals to adopt on Stardoll!

TOP tips

Superstars can even adopt an endangered animal on Stardoll! Hop online to find out more.

Animals Accessorized

The choice of pets is only the beginning. Circle your faves from these accessories you can find at Starplaza!

So Many Pets!

Activity

How many of the above animals have you either: **A)** played with as your own or your friends' pets, or **B)** seen in the wild? Put the total number in the box next to each of them!

Primp YOUR PETS

On Stardoll, we also want to see your creative ideas on whacky new breeds of pets! 'Primp My Pet' is one of our most popular games that you can access via the Dress-ups & Games tab.

1 Pick a pet

Select animal

GO TO STUDIO

TOP tips

On 'Primp My Pet', pick a dog, cat or horse, and then really let the fur (and your imagination) fly! By changing patterns and colours you can come up with new species!

2 Style your pet

TOP tips

You could try matching your primped pet to your suite design!

3 Accessorize

4 Have fun!

JOIN A CLUB!

Being part of a club where you live is great fun, and on Stardoll the possibilities are endless! There are so many clubs you can be a part of, covering a huge range of themes including celebs, animals and styles. There's even philosophy clubs for all you deep-thinking fashion fans!

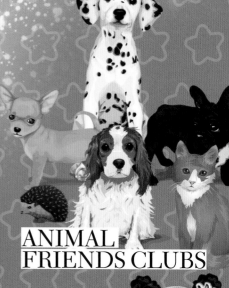

ANIMAL FRIENDS CLUBS

HOT OR NOT CLUBS

ANYTHING & EVERYTHING CLUBS

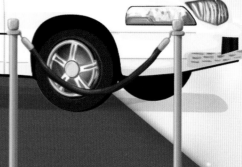

CELEBRITY CLUBS

STYLE CLUBS

MY PHILOSOPHY CLUBS

I THINK . . . CLUBS

MEDIA CLUBS

(Activity) Joining In

Fancy being friends with like-minded Stardoll members and joining one of these clubs? It couldn't be easier! All you need to do is find a club that suits your tastes on the CLUBS & FRIENDS zone and click 'Join This Club'. Then you can interact with your new friends, join discussions and check out sceneries.

PART OF A CLUB WHERE YOU LIVE? STICK A PHOTO IN HERE OF YOU AND YOUR FRIENDS AT A CLUB MEETING!

NOT IN A CLUB? TAKE STARDOLL'S IDEA AND FORM ONE!

.... & CREATE YOUR OWN TOO!

All of the Stardoll Clubs started by a member founding them – so you can start a club about anything you like too! First of all, notch up 200 Starpoints (you get points for all the activities you do on Stardoll, like playing with MeDolls, making Albums and decorating Suites). You'll reach 200 in no time, plus, this earns you a free gift! Collect your gift from your Suite, then you can set up your own club! Click on 'Clubs & Friends', then . . .

1 Pick a club name

2 Upload logos

3 Choose a background scene

4 Decorate it however you like

5 Tell your friends & enjoy!

Activity So Many Decisions

Get together with your friends and chat about what kinds of clubs you'd like to set up on Stardoll. You'll be surprised how many great ideas you come up with if you put all of your heads together! All members can make one club, and Superstars can create three.

Party time!

From joining a party to creating your own, there are so many reasons to have a party on Stardoll!

You get to choose where you want to throw the party, what items you'd like to furnish it with – from microphones to chandeliers. Then you'll get to take a photo of your creation and make an invite.

CREATE A PARTY

1 Go to 'Parties'

2 Select a location

3 Decorate it

TOP tips

What things make you and your friends laugh? A TV show? A funny author? Throwing a party with a theme that you love will guarantee you'll all have a great time.

4 Invite friends

5 Take a photo of it

STICK A PHOTO IN HERE OF ONE OF YOUR ALL-TIME FAVOURITE BIRTHDAY PARTIES. IT COULD BE ONE THAT YOU EITHER HAD YOURSELF, OR A FAVOURITE ONE THAT YOU WENT TO!

Plan Your Own Party!

Your ideas pad:

Why don't you give it a go – practise making an invite for your Stardoll Party! Design something spectacular, and don't forget to write a list of friends you'd like to invite.

Then, hop on Stardoll and recreate your party plan there, and invite your fellow Stardolls along for the fun!

Your invite:

MAKING AN ALBUM

I'll bet you've already got some kind of notebook where you like to keep things, right? Or maybe it's a secret diary or box where you've got ideas, photos and memories all collected? On Stardoll, you have a very special interactive Album where you can be just as creative!

In your album:

● You can keep a massive 60 items on each Album page, so you'll always have plenty of room!

● You can keep different versions of your MeDoll in your Album.

● Celebrity Stardolls that you make can also be stored in there.

● Clothes, furniture, accessories, Suite items – all of this and more can help make your Album unique and special to you!

● Everyone starts with 10 pages, and if you'd like to become a Superstar, you'll get 100 pages to fill.

TOP tips

There are super-cute stickers and text that you can add to your Album to personalize it even more.

It's BLOGGING TIME!

Did you know the word 'blog' comes from a blend of the words 'web' (from 'website') and 'log'? Now you do! And on Stardoll, we LOVE you guys sharing your thoughts and pictures!

FASHION

PATTERN PLAY STYLED OUTFITS
5 days ago • 151 comment(s)

Isobel.Stardoll

THE FRESH PRINTS OF STARPLAZA:

This week's Styled Outfits had us looking through the same kaleidoscope designers used in their Spring collections. **Stripes, checks, spots, stars, cheetah**--- you name it, they used it! Several all at once, even. The style 'taboo' of prints on prints is no longer a shudder-worthy mix, thanks to the experimental, brave street stylers being blogged for our boundary-pushing pleasures.

Aside from seeing the traditional spots, don't miss the gorgeous chinoiserie, Ellsworth Kelly geometry, and insanely stunning giant orchids. Cuts are simple and feminine and call on the best of the 40's up to even the disco 70's.

JUNE HOT BUYS
3 days ago • 623 comment(s)

Isobel.Stardoll

HEAD OVER HEELS WITH PRETTY N' LOVE
1 months ago • 1546 comment(s)

Callie.Stardoll
30 •

Spring is finally at our doorstep, the Royal Wedding is nigh upon us and l'amour is in the air. Cupid's arrow has struck Stardoll squarely in the heart -- we are feeling the love!

TOP tips

Blogs can also act like an online diary – so why not share some of your favourite experiences with your Stardoll friends.

HOT
10 BUYS

TOP *tips*

Here's what the Star Blog looks like! You can read all about all the latest Stardoll news on mine, plus, what I've been up to lately. Come by and say hi – and leave a comment too!

Ideas pad:

....
....
....
....
....
....
....
....
....
....
....
....
....
....
....

Activity

Prepare For Your Blog

What kind of things would you like to blog about? Jot down five of your favourite things to help you get started!

Friends
& fashion

It's what Stardoll is all about! We love that like-minded friends come together, share creativity, and along the way, make even more friends who are fuelled by fashion! Here are some other ace ideas of combining friends and fashion.

Get Together!

Activity

Gather all of your friends around one of your bedrooms, and start sharing what you love about each other's styles:

(Name) ....LOVES ....outfits

because ....

(Name) ....LOVES ....outfits

because ....

(Name) ....LOVES ....outfits

because ....

(Name) ....LOVES ....outfits

because ....

(Name) ....LOVES ....outfits

because ....

Sketchpad:

Activity Sharing Inspiration

See how much fun and how easy that was? Imagine doing that on Stardoll with new friends from all over the world! There are so many exciting and inspiring cultures and fashions from other countries, that you're sure to find looks and trends that you never thought of! Then, they'll help you come up with even more amazing ideas for your own designs. Jump on Stardoll and check out members from other countries. Now list the top five new, exciting looks you've found:

1) ....

2) ....

3) ....

4) ....

5) ....

What did you like about these?

....

....

....

Have they inspired a new design of yours? Jot down some ideas right now, then get designing on Stardoll!

TOP tips

Did you know that Stardoll is translated in 20 languages? That's an amazing amount of new international fashion friends!

To collect your exclusive Stardoll gift, go to www.stardoll.com and login or create an account. Then go to the Gift Card section under My Account and enter this code, before 31/12/2012: RH-ZZSJ486M3

TOP tips

Can you think of how friends have inspired you? Try making something for them on Stardoll!

Contests & events

The fashion world is full of glittering events and competitions – and Stardoll is no different! Like the idea of seeing your MeDoll on the Catwalk? How about becoming the National Covergirl? You and all your friends can take part in these exciting events – and you can vote for each other, too!

First up, let's talk about what every fashionista
wants to be: a Covergirl! Turn over . . .

Covergirl stars

Here's all you need to do to be in with the chance of becoming a Stardoll Covergirl – or even a National Covergirl!

COVERGIRL

Having the highest rated MeDoll of the day will get you COVERGIRL status! So what's the best way to get votes? Dress your MeDoll and style your Suite with your unique and exciting twists on trends! You can even send messages to other members about your latest looks. Visiting your friends' guest books will certainly help turn heads towards your latest designs too!

COUNTRY STAR!

Let's take things up a level. You can even become the Covergirl of your country! Every day we crown NATIONAL COVERGIRLS in Stardoll's most active countries. With all of the National Covergirl winners proudly shown together, you'll get to see the inspiring designs from your Stardoll friends from all over the world!

COVERGIRL
NATIONAL

COVERGIRL

TOP tips

Try designing your own magazine cover with you and your friends as the cover stars!

Activity Cover Conversations

Get together with your friends and talk about which Covergirls' looks you like the most. Then, chat about ways to take their fashions to another level, and try your ideas out on your MeDolls!

on the catwalk!

Getting on the Stardoll Catwalk couldn't be easier. When you save an outfit in your Album, your MeDoll is automatically entered in the Catwalk show. There, your fellow Stardoll members can vote for it! Here are some MeDolls that have graced the Stardoll catwalk . . .

Think you have the design ideas to take your MeDoll to the number one position in the Catwalk Top Ten? Then get creating, and get saving your outfits into your Album!

TOP tips

Remember: every time you vote for another user's outfit, you earn Starcoins. So get clicking, and get earning!

CATWALK

Vote! Vote! Vote!

75

Awesome albums

The design, decoration and content of Stardoll members' Albums have always been so impressive and creative, we had to make sure that you're rewarded for your efforts! Fancy seeing your Album in the Top Five winners?

TOP tips

Other Stardolls can always rate your Albums, so make sure they're super creative and turn some heads!

"I love mine . . . how do I get it voted as the Best Album?"

1 Decorate your Album with a look you love, and fill it with MeDolls that are head-to-toe trend-tastic!

2 Write a catchy, lively personal description. This will help promote your Album.

3 Send messages to fellow Stardoll users and comment in your friends' Guest Books. Make sure you tell the Stardoll universe about your great designs!

Hottest design

Creative design – it's at the very heart of Stardoll – and we love you all getting involved in this ongoing contest to vote for the best designers!

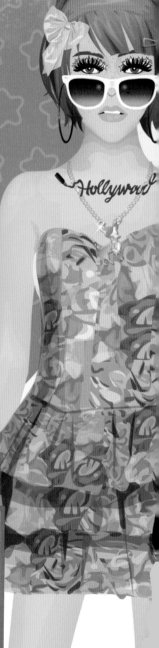

Want to be in with the chance of being crowned a StarDesigner? All you have to do is take a trip to the Fashion Design Studio in the Design & Sell section of your own personal My Page, and come up with dazzling clothes!

Activity Brainstorming

Has a design or logo idea just popped into your head? Quickly sketch it down here so you don't forget it, then jump onto Stardoll and head to the studio!

Ideas pad:

79

Party planner championships

Everybody loves to party, so before you check out these hot party planners, call your friends up and get them to come round! Then you can help each other come up with award-winning Stardoll party ideas.

Party name

✔ Open for all   Your current time is 17:44

Date and time   Style

Year   Pretty in Pink

Hour   Minute

Message to guests

Giveaway   Dress code

Party logo   Create open party

TOP tips

Want to win? You need to have the highest rated parties of the day – so make sure yours looks fabulous! Pop back to p58 for some top tips on party planning. Good luck!

Style
SNAPSHOTS

All users can take pictures using the Stardoll camera. With this, you can save a memory of a special outfit, a favourite room design or even a party you hosted!

Rotate

Just like in real life, you can rotate the camera view and take a picture horizontally (landscape) or vertically (portrait). You can also zoom in and out to get the perfect pic you want!

Usage

Your pics can be included as posts in your Stardoll Blog, album, or to decorate your 'My Page' profile area (your own wall presentation).

Blog

CHECK ME OUT IN BLACK AND WHITE!

Album

Parties & Suites

CALLIE.STARDOLLS SUITE

You can even take pics of Parties and of your Suite. All of the photos you create are saved under 'My Photos' area.

Effects

In the effects shop you can buy special filters to create cool effects on your pics! These include black and white, and glitter effects. All effects have special names, like film noir (black and white) and Copacabana Sunset.

If you want to give your Stardoll camera even more memory (for more space for pics) you can also get expansion packs at Starplaza.

Activity Frame Game

Get together with your friends and recreate some of your fave scenes from films, TV show or music videos, take photos, and glue them in here!

STICK YOUR PHOTO HERE!

STICK YOUR PHOTO HERE!

Check out these awesome effects . . .

Vote me Covergirl

TOP tips

Check out what fellow Stardolls have done with their cameras to get even more inspiring ideas!

Fan fame

We love looking at all the amazing MeDolls and Suites on Stardoll.
Here are some of our favourites!

Activity **Your Faves Are?**
Circle the MeDolls you love the
most, and see if you can come
up with unique twists on their styles
for your own MeDoll!

Check out more of your MeDolls . . .

Fan fame

Here are just some of the members who joined our special Stardoll book club . . .

Fan fame

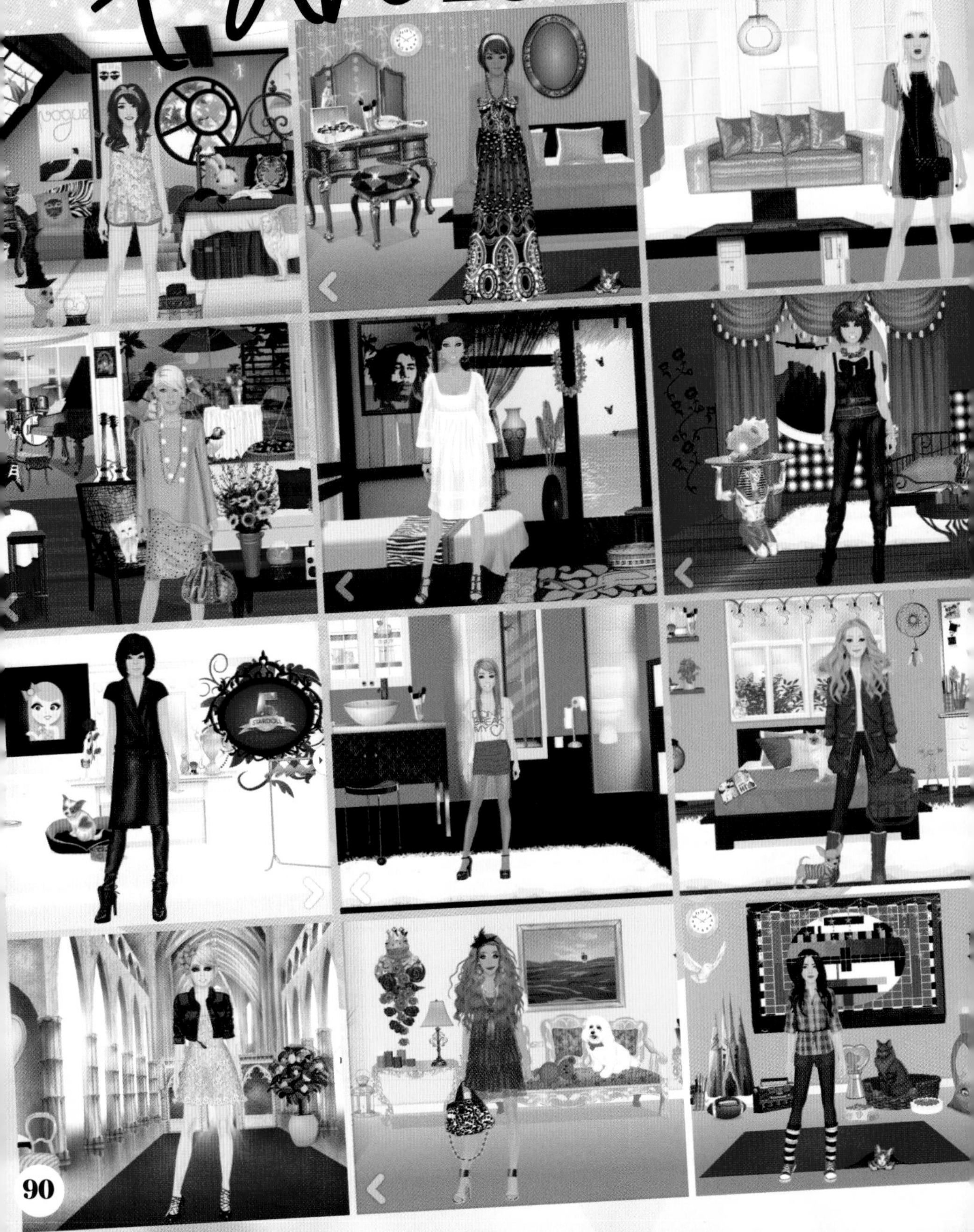

Check out more of your MeDolls . . .

Fan fame

Would you like to be part of Fan Fame next year? Turn the page to find out how!

Fan fame FOR YOU!

Would you like your MeDoll to be featured in one of the official Stardoll books? Keep a look out on the Star Blog for more information on how you can be pretty in print!

In the meantime, keep experimenting to make sure you come up with some truly inspiring and dazzling fashions, furnishings and furry friends!

Goodbye!

See you very soon Stardolls!
Don't miss my blog, the news and
competitions, and get in touch — we
LOVE to hear from everyone and
really appreciate your input, ideas
and feedback. It's great to have
you on Stardoll — have a brilliant
friendship-and-fashion-filled day!

Twinkle, twinkle,

Callie x

Activity Answers

Page 13:
Whose Peepers?

A) Angelina Jolie

B) Daisy Lowe

C) Naomi Campbell

D) Florence Welch

E) Lady Gaga

Page 44:
Different Designs?